Congressional
Research Service
Informing the legislative debate since 1914

Sexual Violence at Institutions of Higher Education

Gail McCallion
Specialist in Social Policy

Jody Feder
Legislative Attorney

October 23, 2014

Congressional Research Service

7-5700

www.crs.gov

R43764

Summary

In recent years, a number of high-profile incidents of sexual violence at institutions of higher education (IHEs) have heightened congressional and administration scrutiny of the policies and procedures that IHEs currently have in place to address campus sexual violence and how these policies and procedures can be improved. Campus sexual violence is widely acknowledged to be a problem. However, reported data on the extent of sexual violence at IHEs varies considerably across studies for a variety of methodological and other reasons. Victims of sexual violence may suffer from a range of physical and mental health conditions including injuries, pregnancy, sexually transmitted diseases, post-traumatic stress disorder, depression, suicidality, and substance abuse. College students who are the victims of sexual violence may experience a decline in academic performance, and they may drop out, leave school, or transfer.

Currently, there are two federal laws that address sexual violence on college campuses: the Jeanne Clery Disclosure of Campus Security Policy and Campus Crime Statistics Act (Clery Act, P.L. 101-542) and Title IX of the Education Amendments of 1972 (Title IX, P.L. 92-318). These two statutes differ in significant respects, including in their purpose, coverage, enforcement, and remedies.

The Clery Act requires all public and private IHEs that participate in the student financial assistance programs under Title IV of the Higher Education Act (HEA, P.L. 89-329) of 1965 to track crimes in and around their campuses and to report these data to their campus community and to the Department of Education (ED). ED's Federal Student Aid (FSA) Office oversees educational institutions' compliance with Title IV student financial aid requirements, including requirements related to the Clery Act. In this role, FSA conducts program reviews of IHEs' compliance with student aid and Clery provisions.

Title IX is a civil rights law that prohibits discrimination on the basis of sex under any education program or activity that receives federal funding. Under Title IX, sexual harassment, which includes sexual violence, is a form of unlawful sex discrimination. Unlike the Clery Act, whose coverage is limited to IHEs that receive student financial aid funds under the HEA, Title IX is applicable to recipients of any type of federal education funding, including any public or private elementary, secondary, and postsecondary school that receives such funds. Although each federal agency enforces Title IX compliance among its own recipients, ED, which administers the vast majority of federal education programs, is the primary agency conducting administrative enforcement of Title IX. Such enforcement by ED's Office for Civil Rights (OCR) may occur as part of a routine compliance audit or in response to a complaint filed by an individual.

Members of Congress have been actively involved in seeking ways to improve how IHEs respond to, investigate, and adjudicate incidents of campus sexual violence. Several bills that would strengthen existing laws pertaining to campus sexual violence have been introduced during the 113th Congress. In January 2014, the Obama Administration established a White House Task Force to Protect Students from Sexual Assault. In April 2014, the Task Force issued its first report—*Not Alone*—and created a website that addresses campus sexual violence. Among other things, the report included an extensive list of actions that the Administration will take (or has already taken) to address campus sexual violence.

Contents

Tables

Contacts

Introduction

In recent years, a number of high-profile incidents of sexual violence at institutions of higher education (IHEs)[1] have heightened congressional and administrative scrutiny of the policies and procedures that IHEs currently have in place to address campus sexual violence. In April 2014, the Obama Administration launched a high-profile initiative to combat sexual violence on college campuses by taking steps to facilitate the reporting of sexual violence and to ensure that appropriate procedures and services are in place to assist victims of such violence. Meanwhile, congressional legislators have introduced several bills that would strengthen existing laws pertaining to campus sexual violence.

Currently, there are two federal laws that address sexual violence on college campuses: the Jeanne Clery Disclosure of Campus Security Policy and Campus Crime Statistics Act (Clery Act, P.L. 101-542)[2] and Title IX of the Education Amendments of 1972 (Title IX, P.L. 92-318).[3] Following a discussion exploring the prevalence of sexual violence at IHEs, this report provides a detailed policy and legal analysis of these two statutes, as well as a brief description of a third statute related to educational privacy. The report concludes with a summary of the steps that have been taken by Congress and the Administration to address campus sexual violence.

Background on Sexual Violence at IHEs

Campus sexual violence is widely acknowledged to be a problem.[4] Victims of sexual violence may suffer from a variety of physical and mental health conditions including injuries, pregnancy, sexually transmitted diseases, post-traumatic stress disorder, depression, suicidality, and substance abuse. College students who are the victims of sexual violence may experience a decline in academic performance, and they may drop out, leave school, or transfer.[5]

There are a number of studies that shed light on the prevalence and nature of campus sexual violence.[6] However, there is currently no uniform methodology employed across national surveys collecting data on sexual violence, and estimates of sexual violence vary across these surveys. This discussion summarizes the results from several studies on campus sexual violence, including research efforts to identify best practices for measuring sexual violence.

---

[1] For purposes of this report all public and private schools that receive financial assistance under Title IV of the Higher Education Act of 1965, as amended, are considered IHEs.

[2] Section 485(f) of the Higher Education Act of 1965, as amended; 20 U.S.C. §1092(f).

[3] 20 U.S.C. §§1681 et seq.

[4] American Association of University Professors, *Campus Sexual Assault: Suggested Policies and Procedures*, February 2013. Christopher P. Krebs, et al., "College Women's Experiences with Physically Forced, Alcohol or Other Drug-Enabled, and Drug-Facilitated Sexual Assault Before and Since Entering College," *Journal of American College Health*, Vol. 57, No. 6, May/June, 2009. Laura P. Chen, et al., "Sexual Abuse and Lifetime Diagnosis of Psychiatric Disorders: Systemic Review and Meta-analysis," *Mayo Clinic Proceedings* 85(7), July 2010. Centers for Disease Control, *Sexual Violence Consequences*, http://www.cdc.gov/violenceprevention/sexualviolence/consequences.html.

[5] Connie J. Kirkland, *Academic Impact of Sexual Assaults*, George Mason University, 1994.

[6] Michael Planty, Lynn Langton, and Christopher Krebs, et al., *Female Victims of Sexual Violence, 1994-2010*, U.S. Department of Justice, Office of Justice Programs, Bureau of Justice Statistics, NCJ240655, March 2013, http://www.bjs.gov/content/pub/pdf/fvsv9410.pdf.

There has been some recent research that has found that the perpetrators of campus sexual violence are rarely a stranger to the victim; instead, they are usually someone the victim knows, e.g., an acquaintance. This (and other research) suggests that victims of sexual violence frequently do not report the incident to law enforcement or campus security. Some of the reasons victims give for not reporting acts of sexual violence include: self-blame or guilt, humiliation, fear of the attacker, fear of how they will be treated in the investigation, not wanting anyone to know about the sexual assault, not knowing how to report, and being unclear as to whether a crime had been committed or harm was intended.[7] Given under-reporting, data collection efforts offer the best prospects for generating information on the incidence and nature of sexual violence, although there are inherent challenges in undertaking data collection efforts in this area.

Data on Sexual Violence at IHEs

Presently, reported data on the extent of sexual violence at IHEs varies considerably across studies for a variety of reasons, including:

- the purpose of the survey (e.g., to identify crimes of sexual violence or public health issues);

- how the survey is administered (telephone survey, in person interview, self-administered computer survey, etc.);

- whether the respondent has privacy during the survey;

- the time frame of the survey (e.g., whether the respondent is asked to provide data for the past six months, the past 12 months, or over their lifetime); and

- whether behaviorally specific definitions are provided for all of the types of sexual violence being surveyed.[8]

There have been a limited number of studies focused specifically on campus sexual violence. These include an often cited 2007 study titled the *Campus Sexual Assault Study* (CSA) that was conducted by RTI International with funding from the U.S. Department of Justice (DOJ). The study reported that one out of five undergraduate women experienced a completed or attempted sexual assault since entering college.[9] The sample included undergraduate women and men ages 18-25 from all classes (freshman, sophomore, junior, senior). This survey was based on a sample of undergraduates from two large public universities.

---

[7] Kreps, C. P., Lindquist, C.H., and Warner, T.D., et al., "College women's experiences with physically forced, alcohol- or other drug-enabled, and drug-facilitated sexual assault before and since entering college," *Journal of American College Health*, vol. 57, no. 6 (2009), pp. pp. 639-647. http://www nij.gov/topics/crime/rape-sexual-violence/Pages/rape-notification.aspx.

[8] Bonnie S. Fisher, Francis T. Cullen, and Michael G. Turner, *The Sexual Victimization of College Women*, U.S. Department of Justice, Office of Justice Programs, National Institute of Justice, Bureau of Justice Statistics, NCJ 182369, December 2000, pp. 4-5, https://www ncjrs.gov/pdffiles1/nij/182369.pdf.

[9] The study was conducted via a web-based survey of 5,466 undergraduate women and 1,375 undergraduate men. Students surveyed for the CSA were asked whether they had experienced a completed or attempted sexual assault prior to entering college, or since entering college. Because the sample of male victims was small, these results were considered exploratory. Christopher P. Krebs, Christine H. Lindquist, and Tara D. Warner, et al., *The Campus Sexual Assault (CSA) Study: Final Report*, U.S. Department of Justice, National Institute of Justice, December 2007, https://www ncjrs.gov/pdffiles1/nij/grants/221153.pdf.

Another study, *Drug-facilitated, Incapacitated, and Forcible Rape: A National Study,* included an investigation of the lifetime and annual experience of rape among college women based on a nationally representative sample of college women attending four-year IHEs.[10] The study found that 5.2% of college women indicated that they had been raped in the most recent year (2005), and 11.5% indicated that they had been raped at some point in their life.

To better understand the factors that may account for the differences in the number of reported incidents of sexual violence across studies, the results of two surveys—the *National College Women Sexual Victimization Study* (NCWSV), and the *National Violence Against College Women Study* (NVACW), both designed to measure the extent and nature of victimization among college women, are highlighted here.[11] Although these are not recent studies, they are uniquely useful in illuminating how differences in certain survey elements can result in very different estimates on the extent of sexual violence. The two surveys employed similar methodologies, except for differences in the number and wording of the screening questions, and in the wording of the questions used for the incident reports. This discussion focuses in particular on the differences in the measurement of completed, attempted, or threatened rape in the two surveys.[12]

The NCWSV asked respondents a series of behaviorally specific screening questions to determine if they had experienced different types of sexual victimization.[13] If the respondent answered affirmatively to one or more of the questions asked during the screening process, she was then asked how many times each act had occurred. An incident report was administered for each occurrence.[14]

---

[10] This study was based on a sample of 5,001 women who formed two groups on the basis of the population from which they were recruited. One group consisted of a national telephone household sample of 3,001 U.S. women, and the second group consisted of a sample of 2,000 college women attending four-year IHEs. The mean age of the college respondents participating in the survey was 20.1. Interviews were conducted between January 23 and June 26, 2006. The study surveyed respondents age 18 and over. Rape was defined as including drug and alcohol facilitated rape, incapacitated rape, and forcible rape. Dean G. Kilpatrick, Heidi S. Resnick, and Kenneth J. Ruggiero, "Drug-Facilitated, Incapacitated, and Forcible Rape: A National Study," *National Crime Victims Research and Treatment Center*, February 1, 2007, https://www.ncjrs.gov/pdffiles1/nij/grants/219181.pdf.

[11] The population sampled in both studies was drawn from all two- and four-year IHEs with at least 1,000 students. Both surveys used a two-stage measurement process that included initial screening questions followed by an incident report to categorize the type of victimization that had occurred. Both the NCWSV and the NVACW were conducted by the same survey research firm via computer-assisted telephone interviews. NCWSV's survey was conducted between February 21, 1997, and May 5, 1997, and NVACW's survey was conducted between March 27, 1997, and May 14, 1997. Both studies had similar sample sizes (4,446 women for NSVCW, and 4,432 women for the NVACW).

[12] In both studies, rape was defined to include: "forced vaginal, anal, or oral penetration by the perpetrator(s), which could also include penetration from a foreign object. Both definitions of rape explicitly refer to physical force and the threat of physical force." Bonnie S. Fisher, Francis T. Cullen, and Michael G. Turner, *The Sexual Victimization of College Women*, U.S. Department of Justice, Office of Justice Programs, National Institute of Justice, Bureau of Justice Statistics, NCJ 182369, December 2000, pp. 4-9. https://www.ncjrs.gov/pdffiles1/nij/182369.pdf.

[13] "A behaviorally specific question, for example, is one that does not ask simply if a respondent 'had been raped;' rather, it describes an incident in graphic language that covers the elements of a criminal offense (e.g., someone 'made you have sexual intercourse by using force or threatening to harm you...by intercourse I mean putting a penis in your vagina....')," Bonnie S. Fisher, Francis T. Cullen, and Michael G. Turner, *The Sexual Victimization of College Women*, U.S. Department of Justice, Office of Justice Programs, National Institute of Justice, Bureau of Justice Statistics, NCJ 182369, December 2000, pp. 4-9. https://www.ncjrs.gov/pdffiles1/nij/182369.pdf.

[14] The incident report was used to collect data on what acts were: (1) completed, (2) attempted, and/or (3) threatened; as well as to collect additional details regarding each incident (e.g., where and when the incident happened, whether it was reported to police or campus security.) Responses to these questions in the incident reports were used to categorize which type of sexual victimization, if any, had occurred. Bonnie S. Fisher, Francis T. Cullen, and Michael G. Turner, *The Sexual Victimization of College Women*, U.S. Department of Justice, Office of Justice Programs, National Institute (continued...)

In contrast, the NVACW was designed to align as closely as possible to the major national survey on criminal victimization, the *National Crime and Victimization Survey* (NCVS).[15] In the screening process, a respondent in the NVACW survey was asked whether she "has been forced or coerced to engage in unwanted sexual activity." The survey did not include behaviorally specific definitions of unwanted sexual activity. An incident report was administered for each occurrence.

The differences between the two surveys in the screening questions appeared to have had a statistically significant impact on their findings.[16] The two surveys generated different estimates for completed rape, attempted rape, and threats of rape; the NVACW had much lower rates for all three categories, than the NCWSV.[17] The estimated annual percentage of undergraduate women who were victims of completed, attempted, or threatened rape was 5.33% in the NCWSV compared to 0.71% in the NVACW.[18] The authors indicated that these estimates would be larger if the reference period reflected an undergraduate's woman's total tenure enrolled in college.

More recently, DOJ's Bureau of Justice Statistics (BJS) has been involved in a multi-year effort to evaluate NCVS data on sexual violence. BJS is currently funding pilot tests designed to evaluate the best methods for collecting self-reported data on rape and sexual assault.[19] Pilot testing of two designs is scheduled to begin in the fall of 2014. The estimates obtained from these pilot tests will subsequently be compared to results from the NCVS. BJS's goals are to "Develop methodology for measuring rape and sexual assault within NCVS; compare the methodology to existing methods; (and) evaluate the quality, utility and cost of the methodology."[20]

(...continued)

of Justice, Bureau of Justice Statistics, NCJ 182369, December 2000, https://www.ncjrs.gov/pdffiles1/nij/182369.pdf.

[15] The NCVS is an annual survey of all individuals twelve and over from a nationally representative sample of households regarding the number and characteristics of victimization(s) they experienced in the past six months. The survey is conducted by the U.S. Census Bureau for the Bureau of Justice Statistics. For the most recent NCVS data on criminal victimization see http://www.bjs.gov/index.cfm?ty=pbdetail&iid=5111.

[16] The authors indicate that "What is unknown, however, is whether behaviorally specific screen question produce higher estimates of victimization in general or only higher estimates of sexual victimization." Bonnie S. Fisher, Francis T. Cullen, and Michael G. Turner, *The Sexual Victimization of College Women*, U.S. Department of Justice, Office of Justice Programs, National Institute of Justice, Bureau of Justice Statistics, NCJ 182369, December 2007, p. 14. https://www.ncjrs.gov/pdffiles1/nij/182369.pdf.

[17] The percentage of completed rapes over the seven months reported in the NVACW was 0.16% compared to 1.66% in the NCWSV (10 times smaller in the NVACW study than the NCWSV study); the percentage of attempted rapes reported by NVACW was 0.18% compared with 1.10% in the NSVCW (six times smaller for NVACW than for NCWSV); and the percentage of threats of rape reported in NVACW was 0.07% compared with 0.31% in NCWSV (four times smaller for NVACW than for NCWSV).

[18] To convert the data from seven months to an annual estimate, the authors assume that incidents of sexual violence occur at the same rate each month. However, the authors note that this is an estimate, since the rate of sexual violence may vary across months.

[19] For the definitions of rape and sexual assault employed by the Bureau of Justice Statistics see http://www.bjs.gov/index.cfm?ty=tp&tid=317.

[20] http://www.bjs.gov/index.cfm?ty=tp&tid=317.

Introduction to the Clery Act and Title IX

Both the Clery Act and Title IX contain provisions intended to protect students at IHEs from sexual violence. Indeed, the Obama Administration's 2014 initiative to combat sexual violence on college campuses emphasizes the responsibilities of IHEs under the two statutes. Nevertheless, it is important to remember that the Clery Act and Title IX are two different laws with two different purposes, but those purposes happen to overlap in the context of sexual violence on college campuses. Because an IHE's mishandling of sexual violence incidents may lead to violations of one or both laws, there has been some confusion about the comparative scope and applicability of the Clery Act and Title IX. Some of the differences between the two laws are described below.

Table 1. Comparison of the Clery Act and Title IX

	The Clery Act	**Title IX**
Purpose	Requires disclosure of campus crime statistics and safety policies	Prohibits sex discrimination in federally funded education programs and activities
Covered Entities	IHEs that participate in HEA Title IV(P.L. 89-329) student financial aid programs	Recipients of federal education funding, including elementary, secondary, and postsecondary schools
Covered Acts	Applies to any failure to collect and report required campus crime statistics and to establish and disseminate required policy statements	Applies to any type of sex discrimination that occurs in a federally funded education program or activity
Enforcement Agency	Federal Student Aid Office at Department of Education	Office for Civil Rights at Department of Education
Remedies	Penalty of up to $35,000 per violation or suspension of institutional participation in federal student financial aid programs	Informal resolution or suspension or termination of federal funding

Source: Congressional Research Service, based on 20 U.S.C. §1092(f) and 20 U.S.C. §§1681 et seq.

The primary purpose of the Clery Act, also known as Section 485(f) of the Higher Education Act (HEA), is disclosure of campus crime statistics and policies. Under Clery, all public and private IHEs that participate in HEA Title IV student financial assistance programs must track crimes in and around their campuses, and report these data to their campus community and to the Department of Education (ED).[21] Notably, the Clery Act requires such reports for all types of crimes and offenses enumerated in the law, not just crimes of sexual violence.

In contrast, Title IX is a civil rights law that prohibits discrimination on the basis of sex under any education program or activity that receives federal funding. Under Title IX, sexual harassment, which includes sexual violence, is a form of unlawful sex discrimination. Unlike the Clery Act, whose coverage is limited to IHEs that receive student financial aid funds under the HEA, Title IX is applicable to recipients of any type of federal education funding, including any public or private elementary, secondary, and postsecondary school that receives such funds.

---

[21] For data on Clery crimes that have been reported to campus security or police, and/or local law enforcement (but, not necessarily adjudicated), see ED's Campus Safety and Security Data Analysis Cutting Tool website at http://www.ope.ed.gov/security/Index.aspx.

Title IX and the Clery Act differ not only in their purpose and coverage, but also in their enforcement and remedies. ED's Federal Student Aid (FSA) office oversees educational institutions' compliance with the student financial aid requirements under Title IV of the HEA, including requirements related to the Clery Act. In this role, FSA conducts program reviews of institutions' compliance with Title IV student financial aid requirements, including compliance with the Clery Act. After conducting a review of an IHE's compliance with the Clery Act, the FSA may impose a fine of up to $35,000 per Clery Act violation. FSA also has authority to suspend institutional participation in federal financial student aid programs, although this penalty has never been imposed.

Meanwhile, for purposes of enforcing Title IX at the administrative level,[22] federal agencies are responsible for ensuring that entities that receive federal education funding are complying with Title IX. Although each agency enforces Title IX compliance among its own recipients, ED, which administers the vast majority of federal education programs, is the primary agency conducting administrative enforcement of Title IX. Such enforcement by ED's Office for Civil Rights (OCR) may occur as part of a routine compliance audit or in response to a complaint filed by an individual. The administrative sanction for violating Title IX is suspension or termination of federal funding, although such a penalty is the last resort, and may occur only if OCR has first sought an informal resolution with the IHE in question.

Both the Clery Act and Title IX are discussed in greater detail below.

Overview of the Clery Act

As noted above, the Clery Act (P.L. 101-542) requires IHEs to report campus crime statistics and to establish and disseminate campus safety and security policies. These requirements, which apply not only to crimes of sexual violence, but also to other crimes and offenses specified in the statute, are described separately below.

Clery Act Reporting Requirements[23]

Under the Clery Act, IHEs must collect and report data on criminal offenses that have been reported to a campus security authority[24] or local police if they occurred on Clery geography (on

---

[22] Title IX may also be enforced privately by victims of sex discrimination, who may sue in federal court. Cannon v. Univ. of Chicago, 441 U.S. 677 (1979).

[23] This information is taken from *The Handbook for Campus Safety and Security Reporting*, February 2011, U.S. Department of Education, https://www2.ed.gov/admins/lead/safety/handbook.pdf.

[24] The Clery Handbook defines a campus security authority as:

- "A campus police department or a campus security department of an institution....

- Any individual or individuals who have responsibility for campus security but who do not constitute a campus police department or a campus security department (e.g., an individual who is responsible for monitoring the entrance into the institution's property)....

- Any individual or organization specified in an institution's statement of campus security policy as an individual or organization to which students and employees should report criminal offenses....

- An official of an institution who has significant responsibility for student and campus activities, including, but not limited to, student housing, student discipline and campus judicial proceedings. An official is defined as any person who has the authority and the duty to take action or respond to particular issues on behalf of the institution."

(continued...)

---

or around campus),[25] as well as data on certain offenses referred for disciplinary action. These data are required to be reported to ED in the fall of each year (through a web-based data collection portal).The Clery Act also requires IHEs to collect and report these data for the most recent three years in their Annual Security Report (ASR) by October 1st of each year. The ASR must be provided to all current students and staff annually, and to prospective students and staff upon request.

Clery crimes that are required to be reported include:[26]

- Homicide:
  - Murder and non-negligent manslaughter
  - Negligent manslaughter
- Sex offenses:
  - Forcible
  - Non-forcible
- Robbery
- Aggravated assault
- Burglary
- Motor vehicle theft
- Arson

IHEs are also required to collect and report data on certain offenses if the individual was referred for campus disciplinary action or an arrest was made. In addition to the offense, information on whether the individual was subject to disciplinary action or was arrested should also be reported for the following violations:[27]

- Illegal weapons possession
- Drug law violations
- Liquor law violations

In addition, IHEs are required to collect and report data on hate crimes:

- Hate crimes must be reported by category of bias, including race, gender, sexual orientation, ethnicity, disability and by two new categories of bias added by the Violence Against Women Reauthorization Act of 2013 (VAWA, P.L. 113-4). These new categories are national origin and gender identity. IHEs must report

---

(...continued)

For more information on Campus Security Authorities, see https://www2.ed.gov/admins/lead/safety/handbook.pdf.

[25] For a description of Clery geography see *The Handbook for Campus Safety and Security Reporting*, U.S. Department of Education, February 2011, pp. 11-31, https://www2.ed.gov/admins/lead/safety/handbook.pdf.

[26] If an individual is the victim of multiple crimes that occur during a single incident, only the most serious crime should be reported.

[27] If an individual was subject to both disciplinary action and arrest, only the arrest should be reported.

hate crimes for all of the Clery crimes and offenses listed above. In addition, IHEs must report on hate crimes that involve: larceny/theft, simple assault, intimidation, or destruction/damage/vandalism of property.[28]

Finally, the reauthorization of VAWA added new reporting requirements for the following crimes:

- Domestic violence
- Dating violence
- Stalking incidents

Required Policies

IHEs are required to have in place a wide variety of safety- and security-related policies and to include statements on these policies in their ASRs. The list of policies that follows includes a selection of some of these required statements. For a complete list of required policy statements see the Handbook for Campus Safety and Security (Clery Handbook).[29]

- IHEs must include a statement of their policies for preparing their ASR, including information on the purpose of the report, who prepares it, and the source of data used in the report.

- IHEs must include a statement of their policies regarding the procedures students and employees should use to report crimes or other emergencies occurring on campus, including a description of the IHE's policies regarding its response to these reports.

- IHEs must include their policies for issuing a timely warning to the campus community if a Clery crime has occurred that poses a serious or ongoing threat to students or employees.

- IHEs must include their emergency response, notification, testing, and evacuation policies for situations that pose an immediate threat to the health and safety of students or employees (e.g., natural disaster, outbreak of a serious illness, chemical spill, and terrorist threat) on the campus. Schools are encouraged to use multiple methods of communication in the case of an emergency.

- IHEs must include a list of the campus personnel and organizations to whom the IHE would prefer students and employees report Clery crimes (however, these crimes may be reported to any campus security authority). IHEs must also include their policies on whether crimes may be reported on a confidential basis for inclusion in the ASR.

- IHEs must report their policies for responding to incidents of sexual assault, domestic violence, dating violence, or stalking that have been reported to campus security or local police. They must also include information on the standard of proof that they will apply to campus administrative misconduct procedures.

---

[28] In a single incident in which an individual was the victim of multiple crimes or offenses, all crimes and/or offenses that were bias-motivated must be reported by crime and bias. The most serious Clery crime must also be reported separately under the category of the crime.

[29] https://www2.ed.gov/admins/lead/safety/handbook.pdf.

IHEs that have on-campus housing must also have statements on the following policies and include them in their ASR:

- IHEs must collect and report information on the dates on which any fires occur in campus housing and maintain a fire log that is available to the public. They must have a policy for reporting fires and for mandatory fire drills. IHEs must issue an annual report with data on fire statistics to ED. The fire report must be a separate report but can be included with the annual distribution of the ASR.

- IHEs must have missing student policies and procedures in place. A missing student notification must be issued if a student has been missing for 24 hours.

Finally, IHEs that have a campus police or security department must maintain a daily crime log that records by date, time, and location all crimes that are reported to them. The log for the most recent 60 days must be available for public inspection. The crime log is not limited to Clery crimes and the reporting area extends beyond Clery geography to include the patrol jurisdiction of the campus police or security department.

The Violence Against Women Act (VAWA, P.L. 113-4) Amendments to the Clery Act

The reauthorization of VAWA included several amendments to the Clery Act, including provisions from the Campus Sexual Violence Elimination Act (S. 128/H.R. 812). On July 14, 2014, ED issued a Dear Colleague Letter (DCL) addressing implementation of changes to the Clery Act adopted as part of the reauthorization of VAWA.[30] On October 20, 2014, the final regulatory guidance on the VAWA amendments was published in the *Federal Register*.[31] The regulations are effective July1, 2015.

Among other things, the amendments to the Clery Act included in the VAWA reauthorization require IHEs to include incidents of sexual assault, domestic violence, dating violence, and stalking in their required reporting of crime statistics. In addition, IHEs must include a statement of their policies on programs to prevent sexual assault, domestic violence, dating violence, and stalking; their policies to address these crimes if they occur, including a statement on the standard of evidence that will be used during an institutional conduct proceeding regarding these crimes; and what primary prevention programs are provided to promote awareness of these crimes for incoming students and new employees, as well as to provide ongoing awareness and prevention training for students and faculty.

In addition, VAWA requires that IHE's ASRs indicate that victims of sexual assault, domestic violence, dating violence, and stalking will be provided written notification of accommodations available to them, irrespective of whether the victim chooses to report the crime to local law enforcement and/or campus authorities. VAWA also requires that officials who investigate a complaint or conduct an administrative proceeding regarding sexual assault, domestic violence, dating violence, or stalking receive annual training on how to conduct an investigation or a proceeding that protects the safety of victims and promotes accountability.

---

[30] https://www.ifap.ed.gov/dpcletters/GEN1413 html.

[31] U.S. Department of Education, "Violence Against Women Act," 79 *Federal Register* 62752, October 20, 2014.

Enforcement Efforts

ED's Office of Federal Student Aid (FSA) is responsible for administration and oversight of the Clery Act. It monitors ASRs submitted by IHEs, and may initiate a review to evaluate an IHE's compliance with Clery Act requirements. A review may be initiated when a complaint is received, a media event raises concerns, the IHE's independent audit identifies serious noncompliance, or through a review selection process that may also coincide with state reviews performed by the FBI's Criminal Justice Information Service (CJIS) Audit Unit. A Clery review may consist of examining an IHE's crime log, ASR, and incidents that have been reported to local police. The review may or may not include an onsite visit to the IHE.

Once a review is completed, ED issues a Program Review report that describes noncompliance concerns and gives the IHE an opportunity to respond. After reviewing all of the information it has received, ED issues a Final Program Review Determination letter. Based on the findings, the Final Program Review Determination may be referred to FSA's Administrative Actions and Appeals Service Group for consideration of possible adverse administrative action. Under current law, ED may impose a fine of up to $35,000 for each Clery violation, and it may suspend an IHE's participation in federal student financial aid programs (although the latter sanction has never been imposed). FSA maintains a website that lists IHEs that have received a Final Program Review Determination from ED. Data are available for 1997-2014. **Table 2** lists all IHEs that have received a Final Program Review by year.

The White House Task Force to Protect Students from Sexual Assault has established a website addressing campus sexual violence—www.notalone.gov. The website includes a map of schools that have resolved school-level enforcement activities conducted by ED and DOJ. These activities include Title IX resolution agreements with ED to address sexual violence at IHEs, Clery reports from the FSA, and resolution agreements and other court filings addressing sexual violence and sexual harassment on campuses from DOJ's Civil Rights Division.

In a May 19th roundtable addressing campus sexual violence that was hosted by Senator McCaskill, Acting Assistant Secretary of the Office of Postsecondary Education, Lynn Mahaffie, indicated in response to a question from Senator McCaskill, that her office currently employs 13 staff focused exclusively on monitoring compliance with the Clery Act and the Drug-Free Schools and Communities Act (DFCCA, P.L. 99-570). These staff conduct approximately 20 reviews per year. Overall, Mahaffie indicated that her office conducts approximately 300 program reviews per year of IHE's compliance with financial aid requirements in two categories: general assessment reviews and compliance assurance reviews. All general assessment reviews also include a basic Clery Act and DFCCA compliance check.[32]

---

[32] For a recording of the hearing see http://www.mccaskill.senate.gov/media-center/video/view/kytv-mccaskill-hosts-roundtable-on-campus-sexual-assualt-reporting-enforcement-and-prevention.

Table 2. IHEs that Received Final Program Review Determinations

Year[a]	IHEs	Year	IHEs
2014	Mid-Atlantic Christian University		Northwest Vista College
	Midlands Technical College		Palo Alto College
	Sterling College		San Antonio College
	University of Nebraska Kearney	2009	Schreiner University
2012	University of Wisconsin-Green Bay		Saint Philip's College
	Franklin Pierce University		Tarleton State University
	Delaware State University		West Virginia University
	Dominican College of Blauvelt	2008	Paul Smith's College of Arts & Sciences
	University of Delaware		University of Virginia
2011	University of Texas at Arlington	2007	Eastern Michigan University
	University of North Dakota	2006	LaSalle University
	College of New Jersey (The)		Ohio State University (The)
	University of Michigan	2005	Miami University of Ohio
	University of Arkansas		Northern Illinois University
	Oklahoma State University		Saint Mary's College of California
	Wake Forest University	2004	Georgetown University
	Louisiana State University		Salem International University
	University of Utah	2003	California State University
	Yale University		University of California - Davis
	University of Vermont		University of California - Los Angeles
	University of Northern Iowa		University of California - San Diego
	Washington State University	2002	Mount Saint Mary College
	Lincoln University		Saint Mary's College - Notre Dame
	Oregon State University	2001	College of New Jersey (The)
	South Dakota State University		Ramapo College of New Jersey
2010	Slippery Rock University	2000	Ashford University
	Virginia Polytechnic Institute and State University (Virginia Tech)		West Virginia Wesleyan College
	Florida State University	1998	University of Pennsylvania
	Liberty University	1997	Clemson University
	Notre Dame College of Ohio		Miami University of Ohio
	Wesley College		Minnesota State University
			Virginia Polytechnic Institute and State University (Virginia Tech)

Source: https://studentaid.ed.gov/about/data-center/school/clery-act#georgetown.

a. A Final Program Review Determination may or may not result in adverse administrative actions, depending on the findings in the case.

Overview of Title IX

Title IX (P.L. 92-318) is a federal civil rights law that prohibits discrimination on the basis of sex in any education program or activity receiving federal financial assistance.[33] The scope of this prohibition is quite broad, encompassing discrimination against both women and men. The statute applies in a wide variety of educational contexts, such as school admissions, athletics, educational services, extracurricular activities, employment, and more. Because Title IX applies to recipients of federal education funding, the vast majority of public and private schools at both the elementary and secondary level and in higher education must comply with the statute's requirements or risk losing federal aid.[34]

The current effort to combat sexual violence on college campuses is derived from Title IX's prohibition against sexual harassment. Under Title IX, sexual harassment is a form of sex discrimination that may occur when the harassing conduct is severe or pervasive enough that it creates a hostile environment that interferes with a student's ability to access the educational program or activity in question.[35] In 2011, ED released guidance clarifying that sexual violence in schools is a form of sexual harassment that is prohibited by Title IX.[36] Supplemental guidance was released in 2014.[37] Although Title IX also prohibits a school employee's sexual harassment of students, ED's sexual violence guidance focuses only on the issue of student-on-student sexual harassment.[38]

The applicability of the 2011 guidance was reinforced in 2014 when the Obama Administration launched its initiative to prevent sexual violence on college campuses. As part of this effort, the Administration established a website to inform students about their rights under current law and to remind institutions of their legal obligations under Title IX and the Clery Act.[39] Although the initiative appears to be focused primarily on efforts to enforce existing law, ED did issue additional guidance to remind schools of their Title IX obligations related to sexual violence. In the meantime, ED has also stepped up efforts to ensure that schools are complying with these requirements. ED's administrative enforcement efforts and sexual violence guidance are discussed in more detail below, following a brief discussion of the difference between administrative and individual enforcement under Title IX.

Title IX Enforcement

As a preliminary matter, it is important to distinguish between administrative and individual enforcement under Title IX. At the administrative level, federal agencies are responsible for

---

[33] 20 U.S.C. §1681(a).

[34] The statute does, however, contain a number of exceptions, such as exemptions for educational institutions that train individuals for military service or the merchant marines or those institutions operated by a religious institute whose religious tenets are inconsistent with Title IX. *Id.*

[35] CRS Report RL33736, *Sexual Harassment: Developments in Federal Law*, by Jody Feder.

[36] Russlynn Ali, *"Dear Colleague" Letter*, U.S. Department of Education, April 4, 2011, http://www2.ed.gov/about/offices/list/ocr/letters/colleague-201104 html (hereinafter "2011 Guidance").

[37] Catherine E. Lhamon, *Questions and Answers on Title IX and Sexual Violence*, U.S. Department of Education, April 29, 2014, http://www2.ed.gov/about/offices/list/ocr/docs/qa-201404-title-ix.pdf (hereinafter "2014 Guidance).

[38] U.S. Department of Education, *Revised Sexual Harassment Guidance: Harassment of Students by School Employees, Other Students, or Third Parties*, January 19, 2001, http://www2.ed.gov/print/about/offices/list/ocr/docs/shguide html.

[39] The website is https://www notalone.gov/.

---

ensuring that entities that receive federal education funding are complying with Title IX. Although each agency enforces Title IX compliance among its own recipients, ED, which administers the vast majority of federal education programs, is the primary agency conducting administrative enforcement of Title IX. Such enforcement by OCR may occur as part of a routine compliance audit or in response to a complaint filed by an individual.

In addition to administrative enforcement, Title IX has been interpreted to contain an implied private right of action that allows an individual to sue in federal court for monetary damages and injunctive relief.[40] Thus, individuals who believe they have been victims of unlawful sexual harassment have two different, but not mutually exclusive, options: (1) they may file complaints with OCR and rely on ED to take action if a school is found to be violating Title IX; and/or (2) they may sue their educational institutions directly. If a school is sued for monetary damages, it may be held strictly liable if an employee sexually harasses a student, but liability for student-on-student sexual harassment in this context would attach only if the school had actual knowledge of and was deliberately indifferent to the harassment. In contrast, for purposes of administrative enforcement by ED, a grant recipient such as a school violates Title IX if the recipient knows or reasonably should know about student-on-student harassment, but fails to take immediate action to eliminate the harassment, prevent its recurrence, and address its effects.

The 2014 initiative to combat sexual violence on college campuses has primarily focused on Title IX administrative enforcement. Thus, this area is explored in greater detail below. For more information on private Title IX lawsuits against schools, see CRS Report RL33736, *Sexual Harassment: Developments in Federal Law*, by Jody Feder.

Administrative Enforcement

Two different federal agencies have administrative enforcement authority regarding Title IX violations involving campus sexual violence. In the lead role is ED, which enforces an educational institution's compliance with Title IX requirements via several different mechanisms, including periodic compliance reviews, as well as investigations conducted in response to complaints.[41] If an individual believes an educational institution has violated Title IX, he or she may file a Title IX complaint with OCR. At that point, OCR must conduct an investigation of the institution and, if a violation is found, seek an informal resolution. If informal resolution fails, then OCR may seek to suspend or terminate the institution's federal funding.[42]

Notably, suspension or termination of federal funding is currently the only enforcement mechanism available to ED or other federal agencies when an agency cannot reach a voluntary resolution agreement with an institution that it has found to be noncompliant. This penalty has

---

[40] Davis v. Monroe County Bd. of Educ., 526 U.S. 629 (1999); Gebser v. Lago Vista Indep. Sch. Dist., 524 U.S. 274 (1998); Franklin v. Gwinnett County Public Schools, 503 U.S. 60 (1992); Cannon v. Univ. of Chicago, 441 U.S. 677 (1979).

[41] 34 C.F.R. §100.7. These regulations govern Title VI of the Civil Rights Act, 42 U.S.C §§2000d et seq., but, because Title IX is patterned on Title VI, ED incorporated Title VI's regulatory enforcement procedures into Title IX when it enacted regulations under the latter statute. 34 C.F.R. §106.71. Meanwhile, OCR's Case Processing Manual provides detailed information about ED's Title IX procedures and is available on ED's website at http://www2.ed.gov/about/offices/list/ocr/docs/ocrcpm.html. DOJ also publishes a Title IX Legal Manual, which is available on its website at http://www.justice.gov/crt/about/cor/coord/ixlegal.php.

[42] 20 U.S.C. §1682; 34 C.F.R. §100.8.

---

rarely, if ever, occurred in the Title IX context, but the threat of losing federal funding appears to motivate institutions to reach compliance agreements with ED.

A suspension or termination of funding must be limited to the particular program, or part thereof, that is out of compliance with Title IX.[43] A school may challenge such an enforcement action by seeking a hearing before an Administrative Law Judge (ALJ) in ED's Office of Hearings and Appeals (OHA). ALJ decisions may be appealed to OHA's Civil Rights Reviewing Authority and, in some cases, to the Secretary.[44] A school may also opt to challenge the agency's action in federal court, but may do so only after exhausting its administrative appeals.[45]

In addition to ED, the Civil Rights Division (CRD) at DOJ plays a significant role in enforcing laws that prohibit sex discrimination in education. CRD has two primary duties: coordination and litigation. With respect to coordination, the division's Federal Coordination and Compliance Section is responsible for coordinating the efforts of federal agencies to consistently and effectively implement and enforce Title IX. In this role, the section "operates a comprehensive, government-wide program of technical and legal assistance, training, interagency coordination, and regulatory, policy, and program review."[46]

With respect to litigation, CRD is responsible for representing federal agencies such as ED when an agency has referred a determination of Title IX noncompliance to DOJ for judicial enforcement of any sanctions an agency has imposed. Thus, the division's Educational Opportunities Section is authorized to sue in federal court on behalf of an agency for violations of the statute.[47] Such suits may seek injunctive relief, specific performance, or other remedies. The Educational Opportunities Section is also responsible for enforcing Title IV of the Civil Rights Act (P.L. 88-352), which prohibits public schools and colleges from discriminating on the basis of race, color, national origin, sex, and religion.[48]

Despite DOJ's role in Title IX enforcement, ED remains the lead agency that administers Title IX with respect to traditional educational institutions. As a result, this report primarily focuses on ED's part in combating campus sexual violence. ED pursues this goal by performing periodic compliance reviews of grant recipients, as well as by conducting investigations in response to Title IX complaints filed with the agency.[49] Available data on ED's Title IX enforcement activities are set forth below.

OCR Enforcement Data

There is limited data regarding OCR's enforcement efforts with respect to sexual violence. As a preliminary matter, it is important to note that OCR has enforcement duties under multiple civil rights statutes, meaning that Title IX enforcement constitutes only a portion of the agency's

---

[43] 34 C.F.R. §100.8.

[44] 34 C.F.R. §100.10.

[45] 34 C.F.R. §100.11.

[46] See the Federal Coordination and Compliance Section website at http://www.justice.gov/crt/about/cor/.

[47] Executive Order 12250, "Leadership and Coordination of Nondiscrimination Laws," 45 *Federal Register* 72995, November 4, 1980. For more information, see the Educational Opportunities website at http://www.justice.gov/crt/about/edu/.

[48] 42 U.S.C. §§2000c et seq.

[49] 34 C.F.R. §106.7.

---

portfolio. In addition, OCR's responsibility to enforce Title IX extends beyond sexual violence to encompass all forms of sex discrimination in education.

According to the most recent data published by ED, over a period of four years (FY2009-12), OCR "received 4,138 Title IX complaints and launched 37 proactive large-scale compliance reviews and directed inquiries."[50] Of the 4,138 Title IX complaints, 1,137 were related to sexual harassment and sexual violence.[51] The figures do not indicate whether these complaints of wrongdoing occurred in the elementary and secondary education context or in the higher education setting, nor is a precise breakdown by institution or complaint type available for the 37 compliance reviews begun during this period. However, ED did report that "OCR received more than 120 complaints relating to sexual violence and launched 11 proactive investigations on sexual violence" over the four-year period covered by the report.[52] Overall, the number of Title IX complaints filed with OCR represented 14% of the total number of civil rights complaints that OCR received during this period.[53]

Although a comprehensive source of more recent data does not appear to be publicly available, ED has indicated that the number of audits and investigations related to sexual violence has increased in the years since the agency released its 2011 guidance. Reportedly, OCR received 11 sexual violence complaints in FY09, a figure that increased to 30 in FY2013.[54] ED has also publicly released information regarding institutions currently under investigation for violating Title IX's prohibition against sexual violence. According to ED, as of May 1, 2014, 55 institutions of higher education were under investigation for Title IX violations involving sexual violence.[55] That figure had reportedly risen to 89 as of October 19, 2014.[56]

Meanwhile, data regarding the duration and outcome of Title IX investigations do not appear to be publicly available, although it does appear that the length of such investigations may vary widely depending on a number of considerations, including the complexity of the allegations, the cooperation of the parties, and other factors. According to one analysis of Title IX sexual harassment complaints filed with OCR between 2003 and 2013, ED dismissed or closed the majority of the complaints it received.[57] ED may opt to make the results of its investigation and any resolution agreement that might result available online.[58]

---

[50] U.S. Department of Education, *Helping to Ensure Equal Access to Education*, Office for Civil Rights, Report to the President and Secretary of Education, 2012, 43, http://www2.ed.gov/about/reports/annual/ocr/report-to-president-2009-12.pdf.

[51] *Id.*

[52] *Id.* at 44.

[53] *Id.* at 6.

[54] Carolyn Penicle, "Campus Sexual Assault Gains a Spotlight in Congress," *CQ News*, April 28, 2014.

[55] U.S. Department of Education, *U.S. Department of Education Releases List of Higher Education Institutions with Open Title IX Sexual Violence Investigations*, Press Release, May 1, 2014, http://www.ed.gov/news/press-releases/us-department-education-releases-list-higher-education-institutions-open-title-i.

[56] Nick Anderson, "Tally of Federal Probes of Colleges on Sexual Violence Grows 50 Percent Since May," *The Washington Post*, October 19, 2014.

[57] Jason P. Smith, "How a Title IX Complaint is Processed," *The Chronicle of Higher Education*, April 30, 2014.

[58] Resolution agreements may be found at: https://www.notalone.gov/data/ and at http://www2.ed.gov/about/offices/list/ocr/docs/investigations/search-ocr.html.

Title IX Guidance on Sexual Violence

As part of its administrative enforcement effort with respect to Title IX, ED released guidance related to sexual violence in both 2011 and 2014. As defined by ED, sexual violence "refers to physical sexual acts perpetrated against a person's will or where a person is incapable of giving consent."[59] Collectively, the 2011 and 2014 guidance documents clarify that sexual violence, including rape, sexual assault, sexual battery, and sexual coercion, is a form of sexual harassment that violates Title IX. Specifically, the guidance notes that a single instance of sexual violence may be sufficiently severe such that it creates a hostile environment that limits or denies a student's ability to participate in or benefit from the educational program.[60] Any school that knows or should have known about possible harassment must "take immediate action to eliminate the harassment, prevent its recurrence, and address its effects."[61]

The 2011 and 2014 guidance extensively detail the types of action a school is expected to take in order to comply with Title IX. In general, a school's duties fall into one of two categories: preventive measures and responsive measures.

Preventive Measures

Under Title IX, an educational institution has an affirmative duty to prevent sexual violence against its students. This duty includes a responsibility to disseminate a nondiscrimination notice, to designate an employee to coordinate Title IX compliance, to provide sexual harassment training to employees, and to adopt and publish grievance procedures.[62] Other proactive steps may include providing preventive education programs and materials, as well as victim services.

ED's guidance provides additional information regarding the role of the Title IX coordinator. According to ED, the coordinator's responsibilities "include overseeing the school's response to Title IX reports and complaints and identifying and addressing any patterns or systemic problems revealed by such reports and complaints."[63] Coordinators must be adequately trained, available to meet with students, and informed about relevant complaints. A school may assign its Title IX coordinator or coordinators with additional responsibilities, such as providing training to students, faculty, and staff; conducting Title IX investigations; determining sanctions and remedies; and coordinating with victims' service providers. Finally, the guidance stipulates that coordinators should not have other job duties, such as general counsel or athletics director, that may create a conflict of interest.[64]

---

[59] 2014 Guidance, *supra* note 37, at 1. An individual may be incapable of giving consent for several reasons, including, but not limited to, being under the legal age of consent or being under the influence of drugs or alcohol.

[60] 2011 Guidance, *supra* note 36, at 3. The federal courts have recognized this principle in both the employment and education setting. *See e.g.,* Berry v. Chi. Transit Auth., 618 F.3d 688, 692 (7th Cir. 2010) ("a single act can create a hostile environment if it is severe enough"); Soper v. Hoben, 195 F.3d 845, 854-55 (6th Cir. 1999) (rape and sexual abuse "obviously qualifies as being severe, pervasive, and objectively offensive sexual harassment").

[61] 2011 Guidance, *supra* note 36, at 4. ED has also released detailed guidance on sexual harassment. Stephanie Monroe, *Revised Sexual Harassment Guidance: Harassment of Students by School Employees, Other Students, or Third Parties,* U.S. Department of Education, "Dear Colleague" Letter, January 19, 2001, http://www2.ed.gov/about/offices/list/ocr/docs/shguide html.

[62] 34 C.F.R. §§106.8-106.9.

[63] 2014 Guidance, *supra* note 37, at 10.

[64] *Id.* at 10-12.

With respect to grievance procedures, the guidance sets forth several requirements. For example, grievance procedures must specify investigative measures and identify the time frames for various stages of the proceedings, as well as provide both parties with an opportunity to present witnesses and other relevant evidence. Moreover, although such procedures may include informal mechanisms such as mediation, "it is improper for a student who complains of harassment to be required to work out the problem directly with the alleged perpetrator, and certainly not without appropriate involvement by the school."[65] In addition, the guidance requires that all individuals responsible for implementing a school's grievance procedures, including Title IX coordinators, investigators, and adjudicators, must have training or experience regarding how to apply the school's grievance procedures and handle sexual violence complaints.[66] The guidance provides a more detailed list of the elements that should be included in a school's Title IX grievance procedures.[67]

The guidance also describes who is a responsible employee that is required to report allegations of sexual violence. Responsible employees are defined to include any employee who: "has been given the duty of reporting incidents of sexual violence or any other misconduct by students to the Title IX coordinator or other appropriate school designee, or whom a student could reasonably believe has this authority or duty."[68] Such employees must report incidents to the Title IX coordinator and/or other designated school officials, although school counselors are exempt from these reporting requirements, and schools may designate additional individuals, such as volunteers in sexual assault centers, as confidential sources.[69] Schools must also provide training to all responsible employees regarding how to report, respond to, and prevent sexual violence. Detailed training requirements are set forth in the guidance.[70]

Responsive Measures

As part of their Title IX responsibility to respond to complaints regarding sexual violence, schools must conduct investigations and take steps to resolve complaints. According to ED,

> ... the term "investigation" refers to the process the school uses to resolve sexual violence complaints. This includes the fact-finding investigation and any hearing and decision-making process the school uses to determine: (1) whether or not the conduct occurred; and (2) if the conduct occurred, what actions the school will take to end the sexual violence, eliminate the hostile environment, and prevent its recurrence, which may include imposing sanctions on the perpetrator and providing remedies for the complainant and broader student population.[71]

Under Title IX, an investigation must be "prompt, thorough, and impartial." A school's obligation to investigate sexual violence complaints applies regardless of whether or not the alleged incident occurred on school campus or off-campus.[72] In addition, a school must conduct an investigation

---

[65] 2011 Guidance, *supra* note 36, at 8.

[66] *Id.* at 7.

[67] 2014 Guidance, *supra* note 37, at 12-13.

[68] *Id.* at 15.

[69] *Id.* at 23.

[70] *Id.* at 38-40.

[71] *Id.* at 24-25.

[72] *Id.* at 29. Under some circumstances, a school may also have a Title IX duty to respond to a sexual violence complaint when the alleged perpetrator is not affiliated with the school. *Id.* at 9.

---

into allegations of sexual violence regardless of whether local law enforcement launches its own criminal investigation. The guidance specifies that schools should notify complainants of their right to file a criminal complaint, but should not wait for a criminal investigation to conclude before starting their own Title IX investigation.[73] It is important to note that the victim of the sexual violence is generally the one who decides whether to file a complaint with the police, the educational institution, or both, although some states may have mandatory reporting laws that require school officials to notify law enforcement regarding certain types of crimes.

The guidance also sets forth several requirements related to confidentiality. In general, if a complainant wishes to preserve his or her confidentiality or to avoid the formal complaint resolution process, the school must take reasonable steps to accommodate the student's request. Nevertheless, because an educational institution that knows or reasonably should be aware of sexual harassment is obligated to take steps to prevent discrimination from reoccurring, there may be cases in which a school is unable to comply with the complainant's request.[74] The guidance discusses the factors that a school should consider when determining whether to fulfill a student's request for privacy.[75] It is also important to note that a complainant's confidentiality request may conflict with an alleged perpetrator's right to access his or her educational records under the Family Educational Rights and Privacy Act (FERPA, P.L. 93-380). The intersection between FERPA and Title IX is discussed in a separate section below.

The Disciplinary Hearing

Once the initial fact-finding stage of the investigation is complete, an educational institution will generally hold a hearing to determine whether a Title IX violation has occurred and, if so, what sanctions should be imposed on the perpetrator. Often, such hearings are conducted as part of the regular disciplinary process that most schools have established to evaluate violations of an institution's code of conduct. An institution may use its traditional disciplinary process to resolve Title IX complaints as long as its grievance procedures conform to the requirements of Title IX.

One such Title IX requirement pertains to the standard of proof that should apply when resolving Title IX complaints. In the past, some schools have used a "clear and convincing evidence" standard, which requires a finding that it is highly probable or reasonably certain that a violation occurred, while other schools relied on the less stringent "preponderance of the evidence" standard that requires a school to determine whether it is more likely than not that sexual harassment occurred. The preponderance of the evidence standard is the standard of proof that generally applies in civil rights cases,[76] as well as many other types of civil litigation and administrative adjudication. As a result, the guidance specifies that schools must adopt this standard when resolving Title IX complaints.[77] As discussed in more detail below, adoption of this preponderance of the evidence standard has proved controversial.

---

[73] 2011 Guidance, *supra* note 36, at 10.

[74] *Id.* at 5.

[75] 2014 Guidance, *supra* note 37, at 21-22.

[76] *See, e.g.*, Price Waterhouse v. Hopkins, 490 U.S. 228, 253 (1989) ("Conventional rules of civil litigation generally apply in Title VII cases ... and one of these rules is that parties to civil litigation need only prove their case by a preponderance of the evidence".); Bazemore v. Friday, 478 U.S. 385 (1986); Williams v. Paint Valley Local Sch. Dist., 400 F.3d 360 (6th Cir. 2005); Cohen v. Brown Univ., 991 F.2d 888, 902 (1st Cir. 1993).

[77] 2011 Guidance, *supra* note 36, at 10-11. Under the Clery Act, IHEs must disclose the standard of proof that they use in disciplinary hearings involving domestic violence, dating violence, sexual assault, or stalking. Although the Clery (continued...)

Final Stages of Investigation

After the disciplinary process has concluded, a school must provide both parties with written notice of the outcome, consistent with FERPA requirements relating to the privacy of educational records.[78] OCR has indicated that a typical investigation should take approximately 60 days to complete, although the agency has acknowledged that this timeframe may vary depending on the circumstances involved.[79]

If a school determines that a hostile environment exists, it must take corrective action "to eliminate the harassment, prevent its recurrence, and address its effects."[80] In addition to disciplinary action taken against the perpetrator, corrective action may include remedies for the complainant. Such remedies may include interim measures that may be taken before the complaint is resolved, such as accommodations regarding living arrangements, class schedules, course work, or extracurricular activities. Schools should also notify complainants of their rights under Title IX and refer them to available counseling resources. The guidance provides a detailed list of the types of remedies an educational institution may wish to consider.[81]

If OCR finds that an educational institution has not complied with its Title IX obligation to prevent and respond to sexual violence, then the agency has broad discretion to negotiate a wide range of remedies and corrective action with that institution. If OCR and the institution cannot reach a voluntary agreement, then OCR may seek to suspend or terminate federal funding. The guidance provides a series of examples of the various types of remedies that OCR might seek if it finds that an institution is not in compliance with Title IX's prohibition against sexual harassment.[82]

Educational institutions should also be aware that Title IX prohibits retaliation.[83] Thus, a school violates Title IX if it retaliates against a student, parent, teacher, or other employee who complains about sexual violence or participates in an investigation related to such a complaint. According to ED, an educational institution must take steps to prevent retaliation against a complainant by an alleged perpetrator.[84]

Finally, it is important to note that ED has clarified that Title IX's prohibition against sex discrimination encompasses gender stereotyping that results in discrimination on the basis of gender identity.[85] Thus, sexual violence against individuals who fail to conform to stereotypical

---

(...continued)

Act does not specify what the standard of proof must be in such cases, it seems likely that schools will adopt a preponderance of the evidence standard in order to remain in compliance with Title IX.

[78] 2011 Guidance, *supra* note 36, at 13-14.

[79] 2014 Guidance, *supra* note 37, at 31-32.

[80] 2011 Guidance, *supra* note 36, at 4.

[81] 2014 Guidance, *supra* note 37, at 34-36.

[82] *Id.* at 16-19.

[83] 34 C.F.R. §100.7(e). *See also*, Jackson v. Birmingham Bd. of Educ., 544 U.S. 167 (2005).

[84] *Id.* at 42-43.

[85] *See, e.g.*, Price Waterhouse v. Hopkins, 490 U.S. 228 (1989); Ray v. Antioch Unified Sch. Dist., 107 F. Supp. 2d 1165 (N.D. Cal. 2000); Doe v. Perry Cmty. Sch. Dist., 316 F. Supp. 2d 809 (S.D. Iowa 2004). *See also*, U.S. Department of Education, *Office for Civil Rights*, Dear Colleague Letter, October 26, 2010, http://www2.ed.gov/about/offices/list/ocr/letters/colleague-201010.html.

---

notions of masculinity or femininity is subject to the requirements outlined in ED's guidance. The guidance also provides information regarding the applicability of Title IX's prohibition against sexual violence to special populations, including disabled students and students who are not citizens.[86]

The Family Educational Rights and Privacy Act

FERPA (P.L. 93-380) guarantees students access to their education records, while limiting the disclosure of those records to third parties. FERPA privacy protections that extend to an alleged perpetrator, therefore, may conflict at times with the Title IX (P.L. 92-318) rights afforded to an alleged victim of sexual violence.

As noted above, an educational institution is required under Title IX to take steps to preserve a complainant's confidentiality if so requested. An alleged perpetrator, however, has the right to review the complaint if it is an educational record within the meaning of FERPA.[87] Under such circumstances, an educational institution must provide the alleged harasser with access to the information contained in the complaint but should, to the extent possible, avoid revealing the complainant's name or other identifying information.

FERPA also prohibits educational institutions that receive federal funds from releasing students' educational records without prior written consent.[88] On its face, this prohibition would appear to prevent a school from disclosing the results of a disciplinary hearing that are part of a perpetrator's educational record. However, FERPA contains a number of exceptions. For example, a postsecondary institution may disclose to an alleged victim of any crime of violence or nonforcible sex offense the final results of any disciplinary proceeding conducted by the institution against the alleged perpetrator. Likewise, an institution may disclose to anyone the final results of any disciplinary proceeding conducted against a student who is an alleged perpetrator of any crime of violence or nonforcible sex offense if the institution determines as a result of the proceeding that the student committed a violation of the institution's rules or policies with respect to such crime or offense.[89] Thus, FERPA permits, but does not require, a school to disclose the results of a disciplinary hearing involving sexual violence.

Current Clery Act and Title IX Issues Regarding Sexual Violence at IHEs

This section discusses several policy and legal issues that have arisen with respect to the Clery Act (P.L. 101-542) and Title IX.

---

[86] 2014 Guidance, *supra* note 37, at 6-8.

[87] "Education records" are defined to include those records, files, documents, and other materials that contain information directly related to a student and that are maintained by an educational agency or institution or by a person acting for such agency or institution. 20 U.S.C. §1232g(a)(4)(A).

[88] 20 U.S.C. §1232g(b). For more information on FERPA, see CRS Report RS22341, *The Family Educational Rights and Privacy Act (FERPA): A Legal Overview*, by Jody Feder.

[89] 20 U.S.C. §1232g(b)(6).

Reliability of Clery Statistics

IHEs have come under increasing scrutiny due to allegations that some may be underreporting crimes of sexual violence at their campuses as required by Clery. In addition, the lack of consistency in the way crimes are reported across IHEs has raised questions about the usefulness of these statistics in assessing the extent of sexual violence and how it is being handled across IHEs. The American Association of University Professors has stated that "While a small number of institutions have put in place rigorous procedures for obtaining, collating, tracking, processing, and reporting Clery statistics, a standardized model for the overall process does not yet exist."[90] IHEs that are the most rigorous in monitoring and collecting statistics on campus sexual violence may report more complaints of sexual violence than IHEs that are not as diligent in monitoring and reporting such complaints. Thus, in press accounts and in their ASRs, IHEs that may be in compliance with Clery reporting requirements may appear to have a more serious sexual violence problem than IHEs that may not be in compliance (and may actually have a more serious sexual violence problem). These potential discrepancies are important for IHEs because press accounts and ASR data on campus sexual violence may be viewed by current and prospective students and their families to evaluate the safety of IHEs.[91]

The possibility that some IHEs may be underreporting incidents of sexual violence, as well as the inconsistency across IHEs in the rigor with which sexual violence is monitored and reported, have prompted some to suggest that more objective measures of sexual violence at IHEs, such as school climate surveys,[92] might be useful to get a clearer picture of the extent of sexual violence across IHEs.[93]

Title IX and the Preponderance of the Evidence Standard

As noted above, the Title IX guidance requires schools to adopt a preponderance of the evidence standard for disciplinary hearings involving sexual violence. This requirement has proved controversial. Indeed, some critics contend that use of this standard is unfair, arguing that alleged perpetrators who are subject to this standard are being deprived of their due process rights.[94] From a legal perspective, however, it is well established that different rights and corresponding procedures attach in the administrative versus judicial setting, and that it is common for an individual to be subject to both criminal and civil proceedings based on the same incident. In general, the standard of proof is higher in the criminal context because more is at stake, while a lesser standard of proof is permitted in civil proceedings because the potential loss of rights is less significant.

---

[90] American Association of University Professors, *Campus Sexual Assault: Suggested Policies and Procedures*, updated, February 2013, http://www.aaup.org/report/campus-sexual-assault-suggested-policies-and-procedures.

[91] http://www.mccaskill.senate.gov/media-center/latest-headlines/why-some-schools-should-celebrate-being-at-the-top-of-reported-campus-rape-lists.

[92] According to ED, "By assessing the perceptions of school climate, educators and education agencies can identify key issues in need of reform. Once needs are identified, data from school climate assessments can be used to set goals and priorities and choose programmatic interventions. Data also can identify areas where students, staff, and parents view climate in similar or dissimilar ways." http://safesupportivelearning.ed.gov/topic-research/school-climate-measurement.

[93] http://safesupportivelearning.ed.gov/topic-research/school-climate-measurement.

[94] Nick Anderson, "Men Punished in Sexual Misconduct Cases on College Campuses are Fighting Back," *Washington Post*, August 20, 2014.

The concept of procedural due process has its origins in the due process clause of the U.S. Constitution, which prohibits government action that would deprive any person of "life, liberty, or property, without due process of law."[95] The premise behind due process is that the government, for reasons of basic fairness, must provide certain procedures before taking any of these important interests away from protected parties. The Supreme Court has stated that due process "is a flexible concept that varies with the particular situation,"[96] and has made it clear that "something less than a full evidentiary hearing is sufficient prior to adverse administrative action."[97] Ultimately, the degree of procedural protection that is due depends on the nature of the individual and governmental interests at stake and varies significantly in the civil and criminal context.[98]

It is also important to note that the due process clause applies only to governmental actors, not private entities. Thus, public IHEs must provide due process protections to students who are subject to disciplinary proceedings, but private IHEs are not subject to the same requirement. Although it is possible that state statutory or common law due process protections may apply in the private setting, the relationship between private IHEs and their students is generally governed by contract law. Under this arrangement, a student who accepts an offer of admission to an IHE agrees to abide by a school's rules and policies regarding attendance. Such rules and policies, which are generally established at the institution's discretion, may or may not include certain procedural protections for students who violate the school's code of conduct. Thus, a private IHE is under no obligation to provide due process rights when sanctioning students unless it has specified that it will do so. However, ED's Title IX guidance does clarify that if an educational institution provides procedural rights to one party, such as the right to present witnesses or have an attorney present, then these rights must be available to both parties.[99] Likewise, although Title IX does not require schools to have a process for appealing disciplinary decisions, the guidance recommends that schools adopt such a process and notes that appeals must be available to both parties.[100]

Title IX Remedies

Another issue that has arisen under Title IX involves questions about whether the current remedies are sufficient. As noted above, suspension or termination of federal funding is currently the only enforcement mechanism available to ED or other federal agencies when an agency cannot reach a voluntary resolution agreement with an institution that it has found to be noncompliant. On the one hand, the threat of losing federal funding appears to motivate institutions to reach compliance agreements with ED, but some institutions have complained that this potential loss of federal aid is coercive, leading them to enter into such agreements even when they disagree with ED's findings of non-compliance.

At the same time, some critics allege that ED relies too heavily on informal Title IX resolutions due to the severe consequences that would attach if the agency suspended or terminated a

---

[95] U.S. Constitution amendment V, §1; *Id.* at amendment XIV, §1.

[96] Zinermon v. Burch, 494 U.S. 126, 127 (1989).

[97] Cleveland Bd. of Educ. v. Loudermill, 470 U.S. 532, 545 (1985).

[98] Matthews v. Eldridge, 452 U.S. 18, 33-34 (1981).

[99] 2014 Guidance, *supra* note 37, at 26.

[100] *Id.* at 37.

school's financial aid. According to this critique, because an educational institution may simply enter into a new compliance agreement with ED if it fails to comply with an existing resolution, these informal agreements are ineffective deterrents that effectively allow schools to violate Title IX without incurring significant penalties. It is also important to note that penalties involving suspension or termination of federal funding have rarely, if ever, occurred in the Title IX context. As a result, several legislative proposals would create new penalties, including fines, under Title IX.

Congressional Response

Members of Congress have been actively working to improve how IHEs prevent, respond to, and resolve complaints of sexual violence on college campuses. This section of the report provides a brief overview of selected congressional actions in 2014 on campus sexual violence.

On January 29, 2014, Congresswomen Speier and Maloney, and 37 additional Members of the House submitted a bipartisan letter to ED's Office of Civil Rights urging ED to issue a Dear Colleague letter providing more guidance on responding to same-sex violence and gender identity discrimination and indicating how it will improve the transparency of campus data, investigations, and enforcement.[101] Congresswoman Speier and 11 additional Members of the House also submitted a bipartisan letter to *U.S. News & World Report* requesting that its IHE ratings incorporate information on IHE efforts to address violence, including sexual violence at college campuses, as well as information on whether an IHE has been found in violation of Title IX provisions regarding sexual violence.[102]

Senator McCaskill issued letters on April 1, 2014, to Secretary Duncan and Attorney General Eric Holder requesting briefings from both agencies on how they ensure accurate reporting of campus sexual violence and accountability for perpetrators and for institutions that do not meet Title IX or Clery Act requirements.[103] Senators Gillibrand and McCaskill and 10 additional Senators also issued a bipartisan letter on April 4, 2014, to the Senate Appropriations Subcommittee on Labor, Health and Human Services, and Education, requesting more resources be provided to investigate and enforce sexual assaults at IHEs.[104]

On April 21, 2014, Senators Gillibrand and six additional Senators submitted a bipartisan letter to the White House Task Force to Protect Students from Sexual Assault recommending that ED streamline and improve accountability by coordinating Title IX and Clery violations that involve criminal acts or physical violence.[105] The Senators recommended that one person at ED be tasked with reporting to the Secretary of Education, rather than the representatives from twenty-eight programs that the letter stated currently report to the Secretary or an Undersecretary on crime and

---

[101] Available at http://speier.house.gov/images/pdf/education_campus_assault_29jan2014.pdf.

[102] Available at http://speier.house.gov/index.php?option=com_content&view=article&id=1413:congresswomen-speier-to-u-s-news-and-world-report-modify-university-rankings-to-include-campus-safety&catid=20&Itemid=14.

[103] Available at http://www.mccaskill.senate.gov/pdf/McCaskillLetterToDOE.pdf and http://www.mccaskill.senate.gov/pdf/McCaskillLetterToDOJ.pdf.

[104] Available at http://www.gillibrand.senate.gov/newsroom/press/release/gillibrand-mccaskill-lead-bipartisan-letter-for-new-resources-to-fight-sexual-assaults-on-college-campuses.

[105] Available at http://www.gillibrand.senate.gov/newsroom/press/release/gillibrand-leads-bipartisan-senate-coalition-urging-white-house-task-force-to-adopt-key-recommendations-to-combat-campus-sexual-assaults.

safety issues. The letter also recommended that ED require all IHEs to conduct standardized, anonymous surveys of campus sexual violence and to create a searchable database on resolved Title IX and Clery complaints.

Senator McCaskill, with Senators Blumenthal and Gillibrand, organized three roundtable discussions on sexual violence that included stakeholders and subject-area experts. The first roundtable, focused on the Clery Act, was held on May 19, 2014. The second roundtable, focused on Title IX, was held on June 2, 2014. The third roundtable, focused on administrative and law enforcement procedures for addressing campus sexual violence, was held on June 23, 2014.

At the request of Senator McCaskill, the majority staff of the U.S. Senate Subcommittee on Financial and Contracting Oversight of the U.S. Senate Committee on Homeland Security and Governmental Affairs conducted a national survey of 350 four-year IHEs, as well as two additional surveys focused on the largest public IHEs and the largest private IHEs in the United States.[106] The survey contained a variety of questions for IHEs regarding their policies and procedures to address sexual violence, including questions on their administration and enforcement of Title IX and the Clery Act; their policies for investigating and adjudicating complaints of sexual assault; the options for reporting allegations of crimes, including confidential reporting; and the types of resources and services the IHEs make available for victims. Among other things, the survey found that only 16% of the IHEs in the national sample currently conduct school climate surveys and approximately 41% had not conducted any investigations of sexual violence in the past five years. Further, the survey found that more than 20% of the IHEs do not provide sexual assault training to their faculty and staff; 30% do not provide campus security personnel with training on how to respond to sexual violence; and 31% do not provide training on sexual violence to students.

Administration Response

In January 2014, President Obama signed a Presidential Memorandum establishing a White House Task Force to Protect Students from Sexual Assault (Task Force).[107] Also in January 2014, the White House Council on Women and Girls and the Office of the Vice President issued a report titled *Rape and Sexual Assault: A Renewed Call to Action.* Subsequently, the Task Force issued its first report titled *Not Alone* in April 2014. The release of *Not Alone* coincided with the creation of a new website, http://www.notalone.gov, that provides a variety of resources on best practices for preventing and responding to sexual violence, information for students on how to file a Title IX complaint, and more. The Task Force has indicated that the federal government is committed to improving IHEs' reporting of sexual violence, as well as improving the adjudication process and enforcement of these cases. This section of the report summarizes the actions that the

---

[106] The discussion above focuses on selected findings from the national survey. The national survey was stratified to ensure that all types and sizes of four-year IHEs participating in HEA Title IV student financial assistance programs were represented. Two hundred and thirty six IHEs responded to the survey (a response rate of 67%). Much more information on all three of these surveys is available at
http://www.mccaskill.senate.gov/SurveyReportwithAppendix.pdf.

[107] Available at http://www.whitehouse.gov/the-press-office/2014/01/22/memorandum-establishing-white-house-task-force-protect-students-sexual-a.

Administration committed to undertake (or has already taken) in the Task Force's April 2014 *Not Alone* report:[108]

- The Task Force has created a website to serve as a resource on sexual assault issues. The website includes information on how to file a Title IX complaint, enforcement data on Title IX and the Clery Act, and extensive additional resources.

- The Task Force has issued a summary of evidence-based practices to prevent sexual violence at IHEs.

- ED has issued a model school climate survey. The survey will be pilot tested and evaluated by the Rutgers Institute on Violence Against Women and Children, and DOJ's Office on Violence Against Women (OVW) will work with its grantees to implement and evaluate the survey. Based in part on what is learned in the pilot tests, DOJ's Bureau of Justice statistics will work to refine the survey methodology and will provide a revised version of the survey to IHEs for their use. IHEs are encouraged to implement the survey in the upcoming school year. The Administration plans to make school climate surveys mandatory in 2016 through legislation or regulation.

- The Centers for Disease Control and Prevention (CDC) has conducted a systemic review of primary prevention strategies for reducing sexual violence and has published an advance summary of their findings. In the fall of 2014, the CDC will collaborate with DOJ and ED to convene a panel of experts to identify promising prevention practices and make recommendations. The CDC will subsequently convene pilot teams to test the most promising practices identified by the panel. DOJ's OVW plans to conduct pilot tests and evaluations of prevention programs used by its grantees. The CDC plans to solicit proposals in 2015 to identify and fill gaps in existing research on sexual violence.

- ED has issued a model reporting and confidentiality protocol for addressing sexual assault cases. The protocol includes information indicating that IHEs should identify those individuals on campus with whom a victim can speak confidentially and should explain the IHE's policy for situations where it might have to override confidentiality in order to ensure campus safety.

- In April 2014, DOJ's Office of Sex Offender Sentencing, Monitoring, Apprehending, Registering, and Tracking (SMART Office) announced a grant opportunity for a pilot test to identify potential treatment options for campus sex offenders.

- DOJ's Center for Campus Public Safety and the National Institute of Justice will assess best practices for investigating and adjudicating campus sexual violence cases and will develop a trauma-informed training program for campus officials who are involved in investigating and adjudicating these cases. OVW will also identify best practices for investigating and adjudicating these cases. In addition, OVW will test and evaluate these practices through its campus grantees, and it will continue to prioritize tribal colleges and universities for its campus grants.

---

[108] All of the actions described in this section are discussed in the Task Force's report -- https://www.notalone.gov/assets/report.pdf.

- By December 2014, ED's National Center on Safe and Supportive Learning Environments will develop trauma-informed training programs for campus health centers.

- ED has provided a checklist for IHEs to use in drafting or reevaluating their sexual misconduct policies. ED recommends that IHEs solicit all stakeholders to provide input in the development of a sexual misconduct policy. Among other things, the checklist addresses ideas an IHE should consider in defining consent.

- The Task Force has published a sample Memorandum of Understanding (MOU) for schools to use for coordinating their efforts with rape crisis centers. It plans to issue a similar MOU for schools to use to coordinate with law enforcement.

- OCR has issued a guidance document, *Questions and Answers on Title IX and Sexual Violence*, to help IHEs understand their legal obligations under Title IX.

- ED and DOJ have entered into an agreement to coordinate Title IX efforts, as have ED's offices responsible for enforcement of Title IX and the Clery Act.

- By 2015, ED will collect and make publicly available a list of all Title IX coordinators.

- The Administration is reviewing laws and regulations that address sexual violence to identify any potential improvements and updating that may be needed. The Administration will also seek new resources to enhance enforcement and will consider how the recommendations developed for campuses can be adapted for public elementary and secondary schools.

The Task Force report also lays out a series of recommended actions for IHEs. For many of these actions, it has provided, or plans to provide, resources to assist IHEs (see discussion above). Among other things the Task Force recommends that IHEs:

- Conduct a campus climate survey, The Administration has requested that IHEs voluntarily conduct a climate survey in the upcoming school year; beginning in 2016, the survey will be required through regulation or legislation.

- Improve sexual violence prevention programs.

- Effectively respond when a student is sexually assaulted. This includes making necessary accommodations for the victim, and identifying trained confidential advocates who are available to assist the victim identify their options and navigate the complaint process (if the victim decides to file a complaint). The advocate is also crucial in helping the victim access needed resources and services.

- Develop a comprehensive sexual misconduct policy.

- Provide trauma-based training for school officials on assisting victims of sexual assault.

- Develop better school disciplinary systems.

- Improve partnerships with service providers throughout the community.

Author Contact Information

Gail McCallion
Specialist in Social Policy
gmccallion@crs.loc.gov, 7-7758

Jody Feder
Legislative Attorney
jfeder@crs.loc.gov, 7-8088